UNTIL THE RIVER RUNS DRY

poems by

KARA THOMPSON

Kara Thompson

Until the River Runs Dry

ISBN: 9781791502638

CONTENTS

HALF HUMAN

With you,
what am I besides the frantic
pulse of the ox, stern and wicked?

The first time I met your mother,
she pulled me aside and said not to ruin you.

What was I besides boisterous
and maddening? I wish I could say more.

Later that night, I walked like an untamed
animal on the side of the road,
high heels swaying in my hands.

In another life I wouldn't love
to walk away so much, but here we are.
The scent of home leads me a long way.

I wonder if being woman is
being part animal, too.
All hoof and howl and
and snarl and sting.

Sometimes I wonder how you're doing.
No, how you're *really* doing.
I wonder lots of things,

and the pulse doesn't stop.
It keeps us alive, the damn thing.

EVEREST

A year has hurried by, but life keeps
expanding beyond sight. Suddenly
I can say I've crossed the monster
rivers, chased miracles through the grass.
But now I have returned home. I can say
I am uncompromising and my own.
Groggily, I open and close the drawers,
the blinds. What has changed but me?
My parents are older, my brothers too.
I've thought of this moment a hundred times,
but never expected such static.
I'm stuck in a wild place no one knows,
caught by the neck and writhing.
A man who climbed Mount Everest twice
in six days said, *Somehow, it's sad*
to reach your dreams, and I wish I could disagree,
but I do what we all do instead: turn in circles
and forget where I come from—heart full of want.

AUTO BODY

The man works on the vehicle and
I would say it is something intimate.

The vehicle has its own anatomy.
When was the last time I memorized

something with my hands?
The man is gentle and skilled,

his hands are dirty.
Is this love or is this work?

To lie under a body much more
powerful than you is thrilling.

To lie under the body of a vehicle is
surrender. And paycheque.

The man is good at what he does.
He cradles the beast, fixes the beast,

knowing everything it could possibly do.
This is honest work. Love at its finest.

YEARS IN THE MAKING

Well, maybe I have been the one who acts like I have
        until the day I die to find someone worth keeping
around.

I'm impatient. I tend to hunk over the fire
of what I've burned and clasp myself tight like
a surviving girl.

        There is a spreading itch, and it runs quick
like water through pipes. It jolts me, challenges me,
and my body
        reminds me of the way I once knew you.

It's been long enough.

Even so, if I lined everyone up,
        I could find you.

I could find you
        looking frighteningly familiar,
caught in the romantic blue light and looking downward,
downward for something unused &
worthy.

ALASKA

I was eight hours north of Anchorage
in an isolated town with a population of 34
and no telephone lines. I felt I must have
touched those branches before, pressed my
brow against that swing, slept on those hills;
that's how familiar it all seemed.
I heard rustling off to the side and saw them:
a moose and her baby calf chewing leaves,
their shapes and noises peeking through
the shady brush a few strides away.
I hovered there, revelling in that wildness,
in the stillness and fear of having a beast pause,
watch me with her eyes and decide if I'm
dangerous or not. Eventually, the mother
tilted her head back down in disinterest,
her calf so naturally and fully by her side,
oblivious. I thought that must be the only time
I've been grateful to be deemed insignificant.
I didn't want to matter any more to her than
a black spruce in the landscape. After all,
we were both there, finding vastness,
but it was more important than that.
It was being assured I belonged there—
like bringing something fleeting back to safety.

THE BIG CITY

I imagined, I always hoped, we would
meet when we had finally been liberated
from our homes, teaching our bodies how
to move in the big city. I hoped it would be
a chance meeting and every moment after
that purposeful. Most of it would take place
at night. The city is so bright at night, and
wild too like our hands when they reach
for each other. I imagined we would be restless
for each other, waking in the morning and
hoping the other hasn't run, at least not yet.
Hopeful is one of the best ways to love.

THE ABSENT

I marvel at the thought of being
two unimportant specks together,

and let myself fester in this
this changed meaning.

We have eaten our spirits
with our teeth,

shared the tough and hardy
parts, and now we know it all.

*

I'm at the hospital.
Peeking through this terrible pain

is another. Where are you now?
My bones will heal before I see you next,

and you will never know how I changed and
unchanged, how cruel and swollen this time is.

As they take the x-rays, I repeat my hymn:
Here you are, here you are, here you are.

*

The canal is swallowed by winter,
left unattractive and hollow

and it makes me nervous to look at.
Where does the life go?

All I know is that it goes entirely.
I sit at the edge with legs dangling,

just to be the one who does so.
Where has this life gone?

*

When I am near enough to the ocean,
I release my hopes for you.

I am deflated, strewn upon a shore
in South Carolina

and what happens next is patience:
long and long and long,

so I creep back exactly where I came from,
my strangeness scattered all about.

*

You are different now,
better at surviving.

You've gone deep inside yourself
and are in it for the long haul.

I trust you are becoming
the person you are supposed to be.

My gut tells me you are deep
in the trenches fighting for it.

BIRD CATCHER

When I'm young I'm wild
without the grief, magic
without the burden.
When I grew up, I wanted to
to catch birds from the sky.
I'd like to say I have. Before
all that, back in the womb
with my twin, I wanted to be
alone. And before that, nothing.
Just the bird in the sky:
hypothetical and imagined.
When I'm young I'm sweet
without the hurt, quiet without
the reason. When I grow up, I want
to be someone that little girls
look up to with wonder and
fierceness, so maybe a bird
after all. Go outside and
put a hand into the sky.
What is yours?

STORM MARK

I rub expensive oil
where it hurts:

the two hips, the sides,
where the electricity gathers.

What a waste of money,
but it hurts to watch

in the mirror, the ripped
skin, bloodless, purple and

grown, I am not five anymore,
nor fifteen and

*(the body was small and the mind
too, tiny and undeveloped)*

here is what I have to say
to the girl:

there is lightning on the way.
Let it stay.

A TERRIFYING PLACE

The world is a scary place to be,
and believing so is no part-time job.
I fret and sweat and collect light
in my pockets, all for the dreadful
vertigo and soft, quiet rage. It comes
at night and my fear shakes me,
hellbent on keeping me alive.
Were we designed this way? We give up
on each other too easily, kick the dirt
like children, unable to find even one
decent thing to say to each other.
We abuse our throbbing hearts
and pick at them, as if they are healing things.
We're forgetting each other already.
What about each other's hands
and how they save us? We forget the
offerings of love that carry us beyond
this place, time and time again.
I wonder what kind of terrifying place
the world will be tomorrow.
Finally, the day breaks,
and me too, just a little.

THE LONGEST MEMORY

In August I thought of you hazily, with no direction and
September was sharp (slashed) into my memory.

A memory: when I stared out the window overlooking the canal
and thought it would be wonderful if I suddenly saw you down
there.
>   Just like I saw myself, walking
>   at any hour of the day.

Still, I thought you could honour this place
as much as I do.
I think you'd love it here   no
I think you'd love who you are here,
who you are as I imagine you:
naming this city yours.

>   Truth is, you mean everything you
>   say and everything you don't say, too.

October is what you don't say: you will not come to the city and
you mean that.
November catches fire: warm to cold, cold to warm. An ironic
cycle.

I still picture you here   (wait for you here)
and the smog makes my eyes water.
That is the longest memory.

DOWNHILL

I tell him: *The world is at its wit's end*
and there's kids in cages so I must be right.

There's a lot of people in mourning but most
of them are not. He says: *I suppose, if you*

really want to think about it like that.
I say: *I do. I do want to think about it*

        like that.

ALMOST TWENTY

I'm coming close to twenty and the more I move the more I forget. Have I learned nothing from living every day?

I need to remember what I was before this, what I was before I went places unaccompanied, before I decided I wanted to see everything.

I need to remember what I was when I cried for my Mother. I'm a woman now, though still catch myself calling myself a girl.

My decisions resemble both. I don't know another way to become a woman besides learning and unlearning.

Maybe in my twenties I'll know exactly where I came from and what I'm built of but years ago

I remember holding my hand in the flame and calling it magic. When did I begin calling it danger?

When was the last time I cried for my Mother?
When was the last time I called my Mother?

I'm coming close to twenty and sometimes when I leave, I don't always mean to slam the door as loud as I do.

Sometimes all I really want is to return to the soft-beating heart. It hurts to miss anything without a name, but I want to remember what I was before I knew that. And I do. I do remember:

It crawls out and I stand still, frozen.

EVERYWHERE

Caught like thread on a nail,
the pain is full and grappling.
A thought of you, tumbling
toward something better off
left unsaid. Only my eyes
can tell you the truth. They
are focused and wide-eyed,
like driving down a dark road.
Bring me something untethered,
something worth more than our
limited days. I am waiting.
I have been waiting for longer
than I care to admit to walk
a street unmarked by you.
To be someone untouched
by you. The wind is closing in,
desperately. Here, hold me out
under the swollen sky with
two shaking hands as a
sacrifice. I am not yours
anymore. Although, if I
ever knock on your door,
come gather me honestly.
Earnestly. With conviction.

BY THE RIVER

One says, *Bet you're a riot, girl,*
and I believe it.

I believe I could
set myself on fire

and stir up something ugly.

*

Tonight burns pink,
and blood is running

like a woman.

The earth is so fair,
and what's done is done.

TIRED FIRE

The sun was boiling us into blisters and
someone was crying.

It was a shame, really, because
perhaps someone had just
slipped quietly into heaven or

perhaps someone had just
slipped out of love, or maybe

there was no crying at all,
just the bees humming too loud

and the cars groaning
and creaking in protest,
filling that whole humid day

like shards of glass in the ear.
I was not necessarily
uncomfortable with it all, but

there were still the unnerving sobs
somewhere, someone holding hurt
as I stared blankly into my
empty hands, thinking

there is always someone under the burning
belly of the sun crying, wailing, weeping.

SEVEN OCTILLION ATOMS

I remember reading that
the average adult is made up of about
7,000,000,000,000,000,000,000,000,000,000
atoms, and don't know if I should
feel bigger or smaller after knowing that.
It's difficult to think of a body as anything
but a completely whole, moving,
spirited form, but what about when
I feel you for the first time? Then
a body isn't just a body anymore,
but a vehicle of complexities,
unlimited matter,
every single particle there,
waiting.

THE ODDS

Would I be admitting defeat if I whispered,
I think I'd like to stay here and not move for awhile?

I think I'd like to live the good life, here with you,
in this thin northern air and endless woods.

Worst case scenario, my insides would rupture.
My own jaw would go slack.

Just in case this happens, will you remind me
this was my idea? All mine.

If I slip into a calm rage, remind me of the fireplace,
the warmth which makes me blush.

If I begin to feel ashamed, remind me of the time I said,
My God, I love knowing a home like this,

with our rain boots by the door, fruit on the counter,
abandoned poems patiently waiting for us.

If I make myself small, cruel, unbelieving, remind me
why I believed in this in the first place,

even with all the odds against us.

WHEN THE WORLD ENDS

Cool hands are
here and   there.

This would be a convenient time
for the world to end.

The morning has come
as it does,
and I wish I didn't know this feeling.
I wish I couldn't put a name to it,
a face.

How do we
keep moving in mud?

I'm so young,
I have so much to learn
about time and hands
and all the other things that
hold us in place.

LUCKY

It seems long ago now, but I still return
to that hopeful, trying time in your car:
my eyes bounced from surface to surface,
your hands, your clean shoes, the keychain
dangling from the hook, swaying with
familiarity. I gifted it to you, brought it
all the way back from the other side of the
sea, held it safely in my palm, shyly and
proudly. It symbolized good luck. Actually,
never stopped symbolizing it. I thought you
deserved the good luck that anyone would
want, whatever that was: abundance,
a great love, you name it. Now I'm far away
and I do, I have a weak moment. I imagine
your clear eyes catching mine before a
world has awakened, glistening with gratitude.
No language, no noise, just a body thankful
for another body, for another pair of eyes to seek
out longingly across the warm space of a bed.
Maybe good luck is what we all deserve after
all, but maybe not. Regardless, I do think we
should all search for it, like animals digging
in the dirt, hoping for something worthwhile,
ready to salvage any piece with meaning.

PICTURE

What ever happened to the gash
of fairness? Of justness?

Don't tell me my aching isn't lonely.
Look around and see.

I see people who carry pictures of the
ones they love in wallets and coat pockets.

Look at all of them. They would jump into
the fire. I wish I knew selflessness like that.

Maybe I do. Maybe I know everyone I'm missing,
and I could recognize them all by a grasp of the hand.

NEW

Clean slate, you say.
You say,
A new beginning.

Okay, I say.

*If that means you're leaving, then just do it.
I'm not stopping you.* I don't say this.

*I mean this in the kindest
way possible*, you say.

Okay, I say.

There isn't much talking after that.
I go out and get a haircut.

And then I take myself out for dinner.
Tasteless and expensive.

I can't help myself,
I just love the

aftermath of it all.

PRAYER IN NOVEMBER

Our mouths were dry, and we had
just come to the top of a hill behind
a church. At the top of the hill stood
a proud metal cross, ten feet high
at least and proud of its stature.

I made a joke about praying to it
and didn't. I turned to her
and asked, *Are you going to pray
right now?* She said, *I just did.*

How? I asked. She looked away and
said, *In my head. What did you say?*
I asked. She swallowed. *A little bit of
everything*, she said. I tried to
understand what everything could be.

I think a little bit of everything could be:
I'm sorry/ thank you/ I miss you/ I see you/
but I can't know for sure, just like I
wouldn't be able to find anything else I
don't know the name of.

WISHBONE

You've sunk into hollow ground in the
nicest dress you have. Oh God,
your mother is going to hate you for this.
Her rage is already pouring from the sky,
though it's always raining in this country.
She hates washing your clothes on Sundays.
She has better things to do like
criticize the length of the waitress's dress
at the diner and do her leg exercises
secretly in her bedroom. She hates
being a woman, hates how demanding it is.
She hates being a mother, hates when her children
run a muck and ruin the dresses she makes for them
with her dry, red hands. Children don't understand
sacrifice but she desperately tries to teach you.
It is disrespectful to come into this household
with muddy thighs when it's half past five.
You're sorry but you don't know how
to say it like you mean it. In your heart you know
this won't matter in five years, it barely matters now,
except it does to her. She is contemplating
how to punish you without making you hate her.
She doesn't want you to hate her,
but she wants you to be afraid of her.
Oh God, your mother still grieves.

OF ALL THE THINGS I WISHED FOR

I never expected you
to rush toward me like
a dog unchained,
powerful and young, to speak
and live like you do.
Before, all the staged
parts of me were finely
tuned, practiced, and ready.
All any of us need is to be
the hummingbird girl:
symmetrical, healing,
beautiful with enough
endurance to last.
But then there was you,
all trueness and metamorphosis
and unafraid of being the
animal in the room. You
were so openly there,
wherever you were,
and I, I was terrified you'd
ask me where I've been and
I wouldn't know what to tell you.

AT EASE

Truthfully, I want to be the one who takes
you home and makes you a drink while you
sit on my old couch, stirring with butterflies
and anxiety. I want to watch you in the cracked
mirror, my back facing you. I want you to break
eye contact and feel something sink inside. I want
you to feel it just because you don't know that
play until you've starred in it. Did you ever have
a fight or flight moment with a girl? What if
I sit beside you with ease and hand you the drink?
Do you take a sip? Are you, in that moment,
reminded of all the ways humans are cruel to
each other? So terribly violent, even in quiet,
soft-lit apartments—especially in quiet, soft-lit
apartments. I want to see you search for a sign,
for something unusual or sinister, for a window
if you need one. I think, truthfully, if it was you
on the couch and me handing you the drink,
I'd want to know what it takes for you to stay.
I want you to know what it takes for us to stay.
Because, maybe, if we tried to leave, we know
we wouldn't get too far.

NATURAL FORM

Do you remember yesterday
when I cried to you?

I said I hated most
things in life and you didn't get angry.

You're not an angry man.
You nodded and were quiet for a long time.

There was a lot of hurting
between us.

I saw you clearly for the first time:
someone who hates just as much as I do.

I felt quite silly
if I can admit that much.

I, of all people, know you are
living and breathing.

I've heard your human heartbeat.
Still, forgive me for believing that this is us

meeting for the first time,
private and honestly.

SPLINTER

In the slight chance I ever have children,
let it happen the way it did with my Mother:
a cold sweat and broken breath in a grey office,
there are two heads instead of one,

Why are there two heads instead of one?

Let it be gut-wrenching and new and difficult.
I wouldn't want it any other way. Let it rain that day,
and let me say with confidence I Don't Want This.

In the slight chance all of this occurs, let it be miserable.
Let it happen the way it did with my Father:
a blank stare and heavy responsibility,
what is the word for a person who can only love
quietly?

Let it be a year later, five years later, ten years later,
let it be the eighteenth autumn knowing that at one specific
point in time, two miracles were made at once.

I don't know a bigger blessing,
this slight chance.

BLACK RIVER

On nights like these I let you take me to the
deep, black river that flows behind your house.
No one knows we're here,
Not even the fireflies or the raccoons, you say.
We are so far removed from busyness that
I can see your breath and sway in such
fine detail that it flutters behind my eyelids.
This life is slower than life in the City,
even more so when we float here in this heavy
calm. This life is slow-motion.
You never ask when I'll be leaving or
coming next. You never ask the important questions.
You just want me to be here when I'm here,
letting you untangle the pollution from my hair,
letting me be small,
reminding me I've been here before.

SHIMMER

When we're young we get by:
eat dinner on the floor,
eat dinner in our heads.
It meant something then,
it meant something to work
for all of this.
It meant something to be
the one with the dirty hands,
the burnt hands.
It meant something to clean up
and impress your Love,
shimmer for them,
because you waited years
for this.
What a wildfire you were
back then,
how bored you are.
Now, you don't owe anybody
anything.

ALIVE AND WELL

At four o'clock in the afternoon, I
tap my knuckles on the couch, almost

in the rhythm of a heartbeat, but louder.
Oh, the way I make life from nothing, how

womanlike, how I give a pulse to slack
objects as if this is my life work,

my education, my passion,
my endless endeavor and I have a

diploma in the art of breathing life into them.
Them, meaning the lamp who goes from off to

sizzling, the chair who sags and sighs, the
clocks who hold their breath before ticking.

At four o'clock in the afternoon, I have
succeeded in moving everything with

the two eyes I own, nothing more.
Other than hands, that is, because

they do magic on their own and
clutch over chests, resuscitating.

The twitch of the thumb, a jump of the
knee. Yes, I suppose some things are

alive enough for names, for brains.

I do suppose, if I squint enough, any

couch could look like anyone and I
do suppose, if I have an imagination,

any heartbeat could be theirs:
thump. thump. thump.

YOU ASKED FOR A SHORT POEM

This body

is a strange country,

aged with fear

and missing faith.

THE NEW LIFE

In this life

I undress and gaze at the window,
        intently watch my reflection:

            my shadow beside the flickering lamp,
skin in its most vulnerable form,
my familiar face and earthy eyes.

I used to be a timid girl, still am
to my core, but I don't care to close the curtains.

There are no teeth, no eyes but

                                my own.

All I see is a distracted city down there and a little moon up
there and

              me in the middle of it all, grown and silent.

I'm better off here.
        At night I bare myself and don't think of it at all. I just
speak lightly and try not to disturb myself too much.

EMERGENCY CONTACT

You love being alone until
it means alone in the city,

until it means alone
at night,

under the streetlamp and
no one around for miles.

You love it
until it's lonely,

until it's barely
speaking.

You love being alone
until it's morning,

until it's sleep,
until it's hand flung out

on the cold sheets, searching.

You love it until it
means emergency contacts,

celebration,
party of one.

You love it until you
can't shake it,

until it follows you home,
until it means craning your neck,

clutching your keys and praying
for just your own blurred shadow.

YOUNGER THEN

The kiss was new and quick,
pushed and pulled between us
timidly. Truthfully, I didn't
know what to make of it.
I was young, didn't know how
to savour temporary things quite yet.
Oh, how unknowing. And him,
he did not realize a girl is more than
lips and waist and breath,
how she is full, full, full.
I did not know much of myself back then
either, had yet to stumble across myself
cracking open the night, teary-eyed.
I had not yet come to be—
a grueling process I must say,
requiring brave sums of patience,
and don't you remember how it all started:
hurrying through time,
even the delightful parts,
so short-lived.

WHAT IT MEANS AND WHAT IT DOESN'T

I'd say I'm a bright woman,
I have some senses and some wits and
let me tell you

there is nothing more believable than when
you're all wound up on nerves and whiskey and
you tell me how you feel.

I believe you like I believe in a punch to the stomach.
There is a hunger here, wanting to be the one
who gets hurt and survives it.

I'm a bright woman and I know when
the time is up.
I've known the entire time. I let you do things
on your own terms and help when I can.

I even go to the store,
buy you the bottle of whiskey
and call it a gift.

SIXTH AVENUE

A man at the bus stop comes up
way too close, swears,

says I have green ocean
kind of eyes and

I wish it were you instead
who gets to see me like this:

in an unfamiliar
place, shaking and there anyway.

MOTHER

My friend, a gift,
she is a thoughtful artist
and strong spoken too.
She wants to be a wife and
a mother. It makes me want
to cry, how good of a mother
she'll be. Maybe she'll let me hold
her newborn, and let me
quietly imagine it is mine
for a few moments. I am not
a mother, but I love this child.
I will wait for that.
Watching her want that life
is one of my favourite things.
I want her to live that life so
strongly it's almost like I
want it myself.
I wonder what it's like,
wanting it so bad.

THE CREATION OF YOU

Was a craft
top to bottom
like a love poem.

All the colours and dips
carefully selected,
and special attention to

the eyes and
to the hands, where the most
gentleness happens.

An honest confession
to form the pumping,
thick heart.

No rage or fire
in such a demanding
endeavour, no, no.

Sighing at the most
mundane parts of you:
the shoulders and spine,

the shadows under the neck.
What a work you are.
You are here:

romantic, supernatural, a thing to digest.

WATERBODY

       If you see a glacier with your own two eyes,
it is melting and it is me.
       It is worthy but it isn't forever
    and those are two different things.
  Find me in the Himalayas, the Rocky Mountains,
          find me in the Andes and call me
    persistent and cold. I don't hear you.
  Over time, glaciers deform because of stress
    from their own weight.
       Find me and call it my fault. Call me blue,
  call me a source.
Find the glacier and call it gone. What do you see,
       really?
   Even the glacier unbecomes eventually,
glowing with quiet and nothing,
     nothing at all.

IMPORTANT NOTICE

Hope is a tiny, fine-tooth comb:

It finds everything and doesn't
let go.

SLOW BURN

I consider leaving discreetly the first
week because your home is right in
the middle of the city. The loudness
is exhausting and I don't sleep much
because the lights outside the window
never dim.

Instead of leaving I learn to appreciate how
the buzzing neon travels over your face
in the late hours, even through the curtains.
It is easier to do this than to change. It's been
a year since I've slept but I don't regret this.

We aren't dying here, but we're here for a
long time. I even begin to recognize the same
voices that pass below our window every night.
Sometimes I want to call to them, to meet them
with my eyes, I'm that lonely.

I never do, because I don't want to wake you.
Besides, the people below could never
hear me; the sirens are so loud in
this city and they go on forever and ever.
I don't know where to go from here.

WORSHIP

Red window
panes bloom. You
rest where it is warm
in this winter heart. I
craft my skin like
church glass for you.
A transparent place, I
am open to you in the
afternoon haze where
your prayers are founded. I
cut shards into blues and
reds, mostly sea and blood
in such a body.
Build me from
ground up. I
make red window
panes bloom, a forgiveness
melting in your palms.
Reflecting in your eyes,
Heaven. Or
the closest you will
ever be. Colours in your
mouth you have never
seen, a mosaic
of me.

BUGS AND HIPBONES

I think about all the ants I'm probably killing just by laying on
the grass. They're suffocating under my palms, my hip bones,
my spine. They don't deserve this. Ants matter too.
They do, don't they?

(I shift my weight and hope I kill less.)

*(I stand up. This way there is a smaller chance of killing ants because
there is less body on the ground.)*

They matter because they exist. And then
take the moon, for example. The moon matters. Even though it
just floats there like a light bulb with an invisible wire, it still
matters. Maybe its purpose is to just be. And to rotate. And to
witness all things,

which seems awfully important and purposeful now that
I think about it.

(I look around and wonder, 'What else matters?')

And you know what else matters? How we carry ourselves
upright, and how we tolerate our grimiest selves, our greatest
selves, the versions of us all to be frozen in time,
caring about everything whether they know it or not.

WORN GLORY

I want all good to survive.
Even the dead things.

I want even the fear to stay,
preserved and reminding.

I want what I've wanted all along:
to allow everything to hold

its own praise and distinction in light.
An untouchable truth:

the glory we find in all things is
worn and personal; the longest lasting love.

WAX FLOWERS

It was such a tender time
and that is my favourite part.
It was never a selfish motive but
I will admit I feared for the change.
And it did happen: bellowing,
exactly as I had imagined.
I never knew better, though I
enjoyed believing I did.
Every morning I would inch open
the ancient window; a ritual for a
believer in the power of a fresh start.
Harsh wind invaded our secret
space but the strangest thing:
I still loved it all so dearly.
The small yellow light and the
white wax flowers at our bedside.
Honey by the spoonful.
Jars of stories, fermenting.
It was such a small life but
made itself massive.
A life is a life is a life. Still is.

MUSCLE MEMORY

After all this time, I want you
to be the safe one. If I could,
I would turn myself in for
the crime of being a girl
while you remain at home,
free yet unfree, praying for me.

THE LIFE WE LEARNED

As a girl, the sun always seemed
to look the same. Now it is a burning cage,
swinging, and I wonder when our time
is up. I say someday I'll live alone,
and the thought doesn't hurt at all.
Is it terrible to retreat, to visit myself
and call the day done? Is it terrible to hold
dearly onto what the good sky has given me,
and shut my eyes to the rest? Underneath
the surface, there is a lifetime's worth
of saying nothing, and another just for
forgiving you for the mistakes
you never knew you made. I can only
stretch this time so thin, so I'll get
to know myself well before all this is over,
as more than just the girl who thought
what she thought about things always
staying the same, effortlessly.

UNTIL THE RIVER RUNS DRY

It means
we know so little
of how this all ends.
It means
I will love you until
it does:
brutally,
fiery,
inevitably.
It means
I want to show you
everything
before we're gone.

Made in the
USA
Monee, IL